Play and Discover
JOURNEYS

Caryn Jenner

W
FRANKLIN WATTS
LONDON·SYDNEY

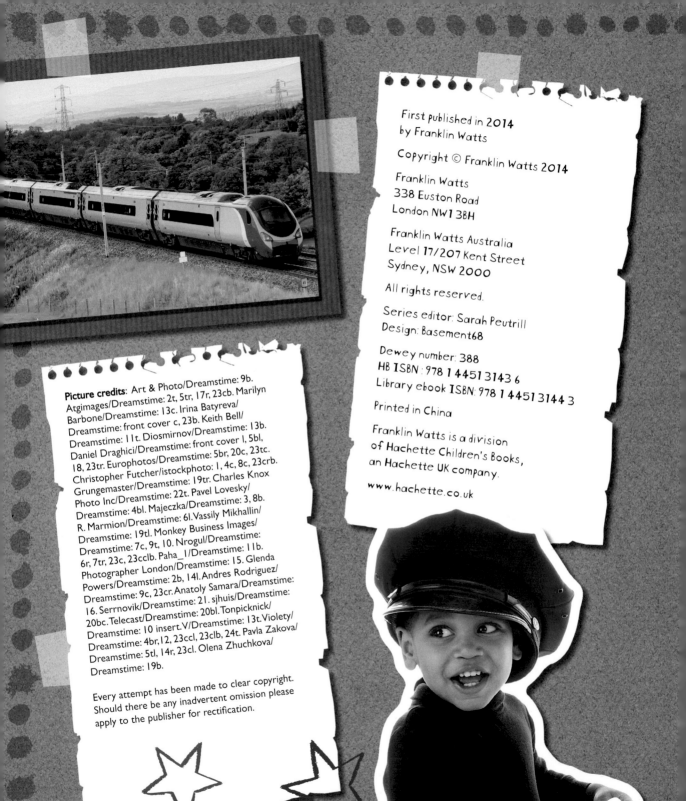

First published in 2014
by Franklin Watts

Copyright © Franklin Watts 2014

Franklin Watts
338 Euston Road
London NW1 3BH

Franklin Watts Australia
Level 17/207 Kent Street
Sydney, NSW 2000

All rights reserved.

Series editor: Sarah Peutrill
Design: Basement68

Dewey number: 388
HB ISBN: 978 1 4451 3143 6
Library ebook ISBN: 978 1 4451 3144 3

Printed in China

Franklin Watts is a division
of Hachette Children's Books,
an Hachette UK company.

www.hachette.co.uk

Picture credits: Art & Photo/Dreamstime: 9b.
Atgimages/Dreamstime: 2t, 5tr, 17r, 23cb. Marilyn
Barbone/Dreamstime: 13c. Irina Batyreva/
Dreamstime: front cover c, 23b. Keith Bell/
Dreamstime: 11t. Diosmirnov/Dreamstime: 13b.
Daniel Draghici/Dreamstime: front cover l, 5bl,
18, 23tr. Europhotos/Dreamstime: 5br, 20c, 23tc.
Christopher Futcher/istockphoto: 1, 4c, 8c, 23crb.
Grungemaster/Dreamstime: 19tr. Charles Knox
Photo Inc/Dreamstime: 22t. Pavel Lovesky/
Dreamstime: 4bl. Majeczka/Dreamstime: 3, 8b.
R. Marmion/Dreamstime: 6l. Vassily Mikhallin/
Dreamstime: 19tl. Monkey Business Images/
Dreamstime: 7c, 9t, 10. Nrogul/Dreamstime:
6r, 7tr, 23c, 23cclb. Paha_1/Dreamstime: 11b.
Photographer London/Dreamstime: 2b, 14l. Andres Rodriguez/
Dreamstime: 9c, 23cr. Anatoly Samara/Dreamstime:
16. Serrnovik/Dreamstime: 15. Glenda
Powers/Dreamstime: 21. sjhuis/Dreamstime:
20bc. Telecast/Dreamstime: 20bl. Tonpicknick/
Dreamstime: 10 insert. V/Dreamstime: 13t. Violety/
Dreamstime: 4br, 12, 23ccl, 23clb, 24t. Pavla Zakova/
Dreamstime: 5tl, 14r, 23cl. Olena Zhuchkova/
Dreamstime: 19b.

Every attempt has been made to clear copyright.
Should there be any inadvertent omission please
apply to the publisher for rectification.

Contents

Go on a journey! 4

Stop and go 6

Let's go for a walk 8

Roads 10

Make a car 12

I'm a bus driver 14

Here comes a train 16

Float a boat 18

Fly an aeroplane 20

With your friends 22

Word bank 23

Index and Notes for parents and teachers 24

Go on a journey!

There are lots of different ways to get from one place to another.

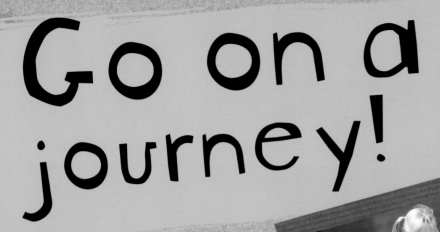

Walk

Scooter

Car

4

Bus

Train

Boat

Aeroplane

Stop and go

Red light means stop.
Everybody stop!

Green light
means go.
Go, go, go!

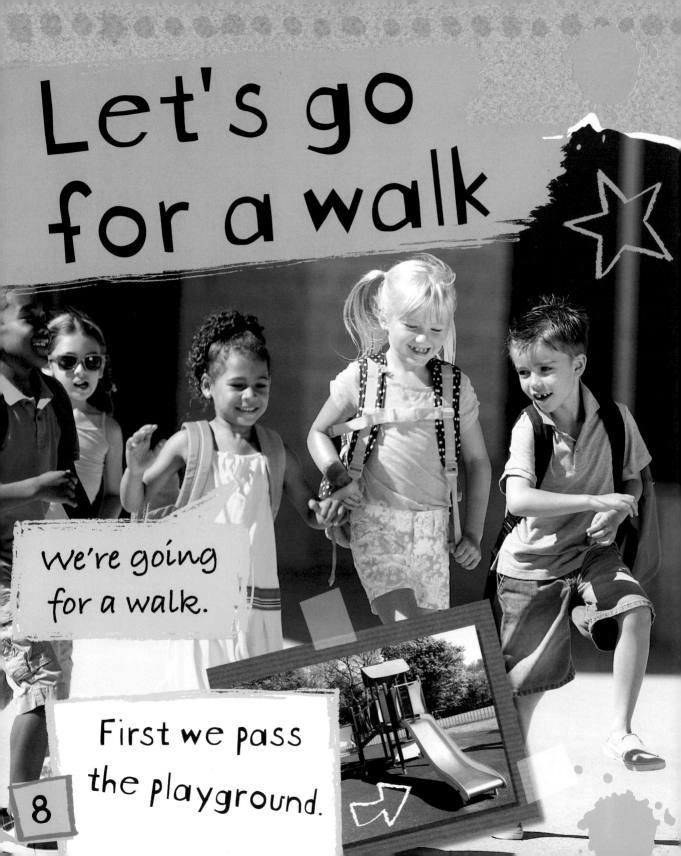

Let's go for a walk

We're going for a walk.

First we pass the playground.

8

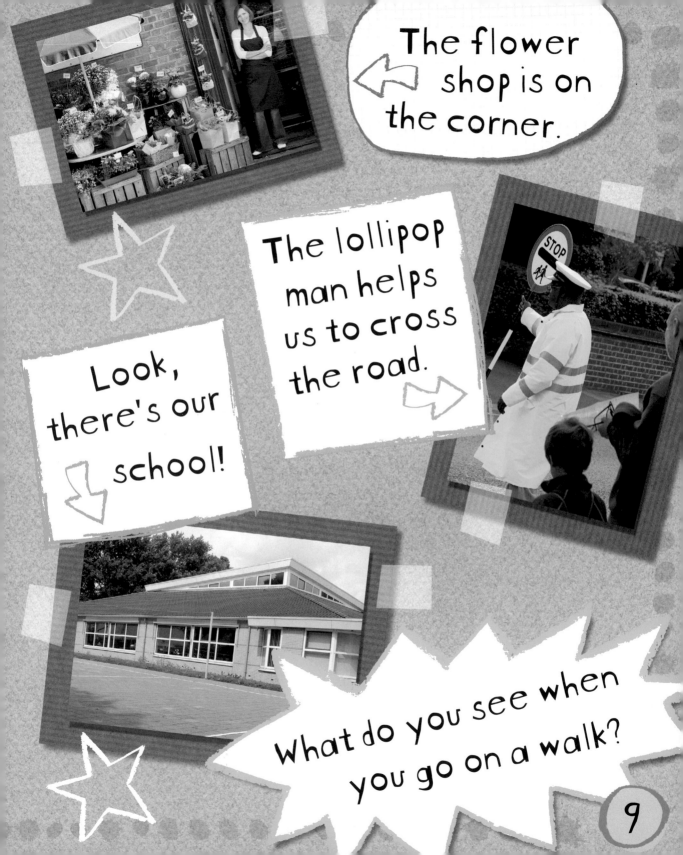

The flower shop is on the corner.

The lollipop man helps us to cross the road.

Look, there's our school!

What do you see when you go on a walk?

9

Roads

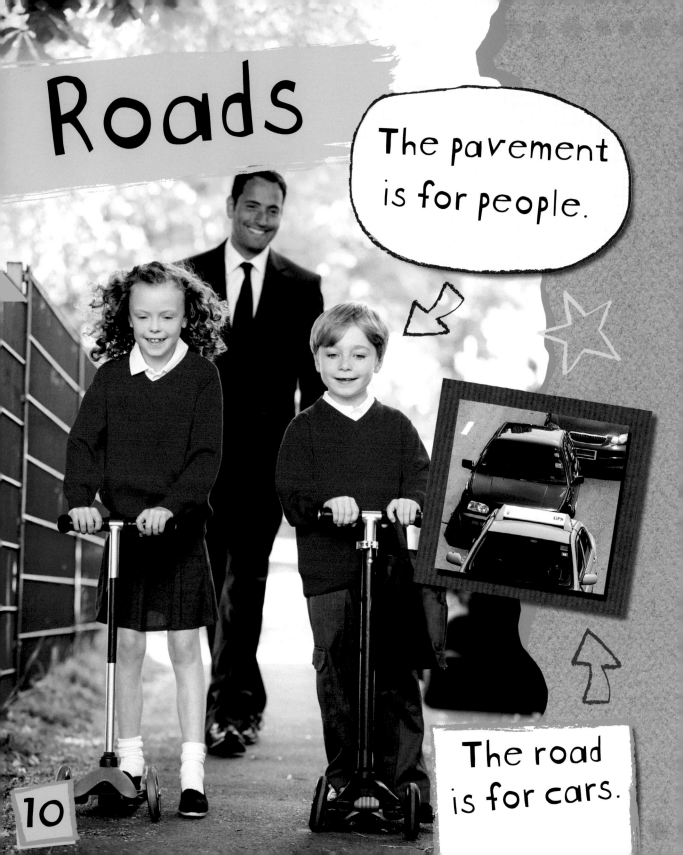

The pavement is for people.

The road is for cars.

10

We take some felt-tip pens and a big box...

and make our own car! We're very careful drivers.

I'm a bus driver

I'm a bus driver.
This is my bus.
Do you know a
song about a bus?

The wheels on
the bus go
round and round.

The driver of the bus says, 'Climb aboard, please.'

The people on the bus get on and off.

15

Look, we're a train. I'm the engine and my friends are the carriages.

The engine is at the front of the train. That's where the driver sits.

Float a boat

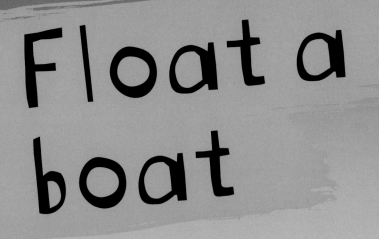

A boat floats on the water.

My boat floats
on the water too.
It's sailing away!

19

Fly an aeroplane

An aeroplane has wings to help it fly high in the sky.

I fold some paper and make my own aeroplane. It has wings too.

With your friends

Pretend journeys

Sit in a circle with your friends. The first child stands up and says where he wants to go on a pretend journey and how he would get there. For example, 'I'm going to the seaside on a train.' The child pretends to chug along like a train as he goes around the outside of the circle. Another child might say 'I'm going to the jungle on a boat,' and pretend to row a boat, or 'I'm going to my grandma's house on an aeroplane,' and spread her arms like wings pretending to fly. Make sure each child has a turn.

Word bank

aeroplane   boat

bus   car   go   pavement

road   stop   train   walk

Index

aeroplanes 5, 20, 21, 22, 23
boats 5, 18, 19, 22, 23
buses 5, 14, 15, 23
cars 4, 10, 11, 12, 13, 23

drivers 13, 15, 17
green light 7
pavements 10, 23
red light 6
roads 10, 11, 23

scooter 4
trains 5, 16, 17, 22, 23
walking 4, 8, 9, 23
wheels 14

Notes for parents and teachers

Stop and go – Play a lively game to teach children about traffic lights. Stand at one end of the play area with the children at the other end. When you call out 'Green light!' the children run towards you. But when you call out 'Red light!' the children stop. Those who don't stop must go back to the start. They could also hold up red and green circles. Let the children take turns being the traffic light too.

Walking – Take the children for a walk around the local area. Encourage them to notice landmarks that you pass along the way. When you return, ask the children to recall what they passed on the walk and in what order. Discuss landmarks that they pass on other familiar journeys, for instance, from home to school.

Roads – Show the children how to follow road safety rules by using toy people and cars. First, cover a table with large sheets of paper and secure with sticky tape. Make road markings on the paper, being sure to include pavements too. Then use the toys to discuss road safety with the children.

Cars – Let children make their own pretend cars using big boxes. Draw four wheels on the box with felt-tip pens. You can also add other parts of the car, such as doors or wing mirrors. Cut out a round piece of card or use a paper plate for the children to use as a steering wheel, then off they go!

Buses – Role play taking a journey on a bus. Position chairs in rows to make the pretend bus. Let the children take turns being the bus driver. Sing 'The Wheels on the Bus' together as you all do the actions. The children could even make up new verses for the song.

Trains – Ask all the children to make a train. Line them up so they are each holding on to the shoulders of the child in front. Then they can chugga-chugga-choo-choo all around. Make sure they all take turns to be the engine at the front!

Boats – Help the children to make toy boats using plastic tubs. (An empty margarine container is ideal.) Stick a paper triangle onto a lolly stick to make the sail and stick the sail into the plastic tub. Fill washing-up bowls with water so the children can sail their boats. Explore making the boats move by blowing on them.

Aeroplanes – Have fun flying paper aeroplanes! Fold a sheet of A4 paper in half lengthwise. Open and fold two corners, then fold again to make the wings. (See page 20 for reference.) Take the children outside to fly their paper aeroplanes. What else can they think of that has wings and flies in the sky?